MW00570849

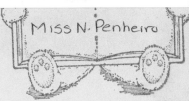

Miss N. Penheiro

The Terrible Finn MacCoul

Story by Tom Harpur

Illustrations by Linda Hendry

TORONTO OXFORD NEW YORK

OXFORD UNIVERSITY PRESS

1990

NOTE:

The Irish legends about Finn MacCoul have come down orally in widely varied forms. This version of this story was told to me by my father and to him by his, etc. I am the first of the clan to be born out of Ireland.

T.W.H.

Once upon a time, long ago, there lived two giants.

Their names were Finn MacCoul and Fergus.

Fergus was master of a wild, rocky part of northern Scotland. He had a bushy, red beard and carried a big club. Fergus was a wise ruler in many ways, but he was so fierce-looking and so fond of fighting that his people were quite frightened of him. So were all the people of the other countries nearby.

1

The one who was most afraid of all — though he never told anyone except his wife — was the other giant in our story, Finn MacCoul himself.

Finn MacCoul was the tallest giant in all Ireland. He, too, was very ferocious-looking with his flaxen hair, his huge sword and shield, his hip-boots and his flowing beard. But he was not really a fighter at all. In fact, the very thought of fighting always made him feel quite ill. He hated the idea of hurting anyone — especially if there was a danger that he might get hurt himself! He never had to fight to get people to obey him. All he had to do was roar at them with a voice like thunder and they never even stopped to ask questions.

Finn MacCoul, in spite of his size then, was really a very gentle giant. He liked nothing better than to stride around the countryside looking at the rich, green fields with their herds of cows, and talking to the farmers about their crops. He loved his castle by the sea and the sound of the waves at night when he was snug in his bed.

He was very proud of his young son, Ossian, but his greatest joy was his wife Sara. According to Finn, Sara MacCoul was the prettiest and cleverest woman in the land.

Now, one evening, just as Finn was tasting a fresh batch of Sara's Irish scones, a messenger from the King of Ireland came riding up to the castle gates with some very bad news.

He told Finn that some fishermen had seen Fergus busily building what looked like a stone bridge across the Irish sea.

"They say it looks as if Fergus plans to come across to Ireland and attack us," the messenger continued.

"The King is afraid Fergus is going to make us all a part of his realm. He says you must fight him and chase him away or we're done for."

The part of Finn's face that you could see above his beard went very pale. His hands and his eyebrows shook and soon his whole body began to shiver with fear. With a soft whisper instead of his usual deep voice, he told the messenger to go away. As soon as he was out of sight, Finn MacCoul, the tallest giant in the land, ran to Sara in absolute terror.

"What am I going to do?" he stammered. "This is terrible, just terrible. I've heard all about Fergus. I don't want to fight him. I can't do it! Somebody — maybe myself — could get badly hurt. I won't be able to stand up to him and then everyone will know what a coward I am. The King and all the people will blame me if the kingdom falls."

His voice got louder and louder. "Ooooooooh!" he roared. The castle itself shook at the sound and frightened pigeons flew from the turrets in all directions.

Now Sara, who was very shrewd and alert in all emergencies, did her best to soothe him and calm his fears. It was no easy task, but when at last he stopped his fuming and fussing, she gave him some hot tea in a cup as big as a bowl.

"There, there," she said, "that's quite enough noise for now, dear. Drink up your tea and leave the worrying about this Fergus fellow to me. When it comes to fighting, you know, brains are better than muscles every time."

When Finn asked his wife what she was going to do, she would tell him nothing. All she said was, "Just leave it all up to me, now. I'm sure I will think of something."

The very next day, the worst happened.

Finn was just starting his breakfast of ten fried eggs, half a ham and a dozen scones, when there was a thunderous knocking on the castle door.

"Finn MacCoul!" rumbled a voice as loud as a cannon shot. "I'm Fergus from across the sea. Come out and fight, for I have vowed to conquer you and take Ireland from your King this very day."

Poor Finn MacCoul was so terrified that he began to tremble all over. He left his tea and ran to the window where he peeked out from behind the curtain. When he looked down and saw how big Fergus was with his huge club and angry scowl, it was all he could do to keep from running down to the deepest dungeon in the castle to hide.

But Sara grabbed him by his arm and said, "Come on with me, MacCoul. We've only got a few minutes before that loud bully down there comes crashing in to find you here. Hurry!"

Mrs. MacCoul tugged him quickly along the stone corridors until they came to the door of their son's nursery. As usual, little Ossian was out with his nurse for his morning walk in the fresh sea air.

To Finn's surprise, Sara pointed to the large, wooden cradle in the middle of the baby's room and whispered to him, "Go on, get in there and pull those covers right over your chin. You must hide all your clothes and that beard of yours as well."

Finn protested hotly. "I'll never fit in there in a thousand years! What on earth do you think you're doing, anyway?"

But his wife paid no attention. Pushing and pulling at him, she finally got him to climb in. Then she fixed the bedding the way she wanted it. When Finn pointed to the huge bumps caused by his bent knees, Sara heaped a thick comforter on top of them. Then before he could utter another word, she stuffed the baby's soother into Finn's mouth and said, "Now you just lie there quietly and say nothing, no matter what happens."

Then Sara ran to open the front door before Fergus broke it down. Pulling the door back, she glared at the unwelcome visitor and said, "I don't know who you are, but you sure are going to be in a lot of trouble if you don't get out of here. Go back to wherever you came from at once!"

Before the surprised Fergus could reply, she went on. "My husband, the fiercest giant in all Ireland, is known far and wide as The Terrible Finn MacCoul. He'll soon be coming home from his early morning walk. If he sees you here making such a dreadful noise and talking about fighting him, he'll knock you down and pull out your beard with his bare hands. Take my advice; start running for home now and don't look back."

Well, Fergus felt a little disturbed when he heard Mrs. MacCoul talking like that. He expected to have a fight with Finn MacCoul, but nobody had told him that the Irish giant was so keen to do battle. However, he thought to himself, "Perhaps she's just trying to scare me off so that I'll leave her husband alone." So, he turned to Sara and said rudely, "I think I'll come in and sit a bit while I wait for him to get back."

Sara gave a big sigh and said, "Well don't say I didn't warn you. I shudder to think what will happen when he finds you here."

So she told Fergus to sit down in the corner on "Finn's wee stool," as she called it, while she whipped up a batch of fresh scones. "This might be the last meal you'll ever have," she told him. "You might as well enjoy yourself now."

Fergus blinked a little when he saw the enormous bench by the fireplace. It was made of solid oak and was the biggest seat he had ever seen. He thought, "That Finn MacCoul must be some size if he calls that a wee stool!"

While he sat and worried a bit about this, Finn's wife got out her
baking things and made some large, flat scones. When she was sure
that Fergus was busy looking at one of the many cats that were curled
up near the fire, she quickly took some of the iron griddles she used
for baking potato bread. She slipped one into the dough of each
scone. Then she put them into the oven.

When the scones were all baked and brown, she made some tea in a big milk bucket and offered it to Fergus. "You can use this cup seeing that Finn's not here yet," she said. "He says it's his favourite teeny mug."

"What's that you say?" cried Fergus as he burned his lip on the hot edge of the tin pail. How can anybody call a bucket a teeny mug? That's ridiculous!"

But even as he said this, he felt another pang of worry in his stomach. Sara MacCoul said nothing, but with a wide smile, she offered him the scones and a pot of strawberry jam. "Try one of these," she said. "These are my husband's favourite treat."

Fergus opened his mouth and took a great bite. When his teeth hit the iron griddle inside, he roared, "Ow! Ow! Ow! I've broken my teeth on this horrid, hard bun!" And to be sure, he had indeed broken his two front teeth.

Now he was more worried than ever. In fact, he was beginning to feel very afraid. "I've got to get out of here," he said to himself. "If Finn MacCoul can eat scones as hard as that, he must be the strongest giant alive."

He got up quickly, bowed politely and, trying to sound calm, he said, "You know, I think I'll come back another time. I just remembered something I have to do back home. By the way, that's really lovely bread you bake. I was only fooling when I said it was a little tough."

"What's your big hurry, now?" asked Sara. "Just you sit yourself down again and have a few more of my scones. You haven't eaten enough to keep a fly alive. Why, my Finn could eat a dozen or so of these as a snack before supper!"

That only made Fergus more frightened. He couldn't wait to get out of there and on his way back over his stone bridge to Scotland. As he headed for the stairway to the front door, Mrs. MacCoul stood in his way and asked, "Why all the big rush? Why don't you at least come and see the baby before you go?"

Fergus didn't like babies very much, and he was afraid it might be too late to escape if he waited around any longer. But he didn't want Mrs. MacCoul to suspect he was afraid. So, reluctantly, he let her lead him to the nursery.

"I'll stay for a minute and no more," he said. "I forgot to close the barnyard gate at my castle and the cows will be eating up the garden by now. I must get home."

When the nursery door was opened and he saw what was supposed
to be the baby in the cradle, Fergus couldn't believe his eyes.

"If that is the baby," he said in a hoarse voice, "your husband must
be the biggest giant in the entire world!"

Finn's wife smiled proudly. "We love the child dearly even though
Finn says he's a bit small for his age."

Terrified by now, Fergus wanted desperately to leave. But Sara went on. "Come here and feel his new tooth. The wee darling just got it this morning."

The giant, who was ready to do anything to get away, pulled out the soother and popped his fingers into Finn's mouth.

As soon as he did that, Finn MacCoul bit him just hard enough to give him the fright of his life.

"Ouch! Ouch!" cried Fergus as he pulled his fingers out and started to run. "That's the last straw. I'm off!"

Finn and his wife listened and waited as Fergus thumped down the stairs.

They heard him bang the outside doors and gates.

They waited as he ran off, still bellowing, towards the sea.

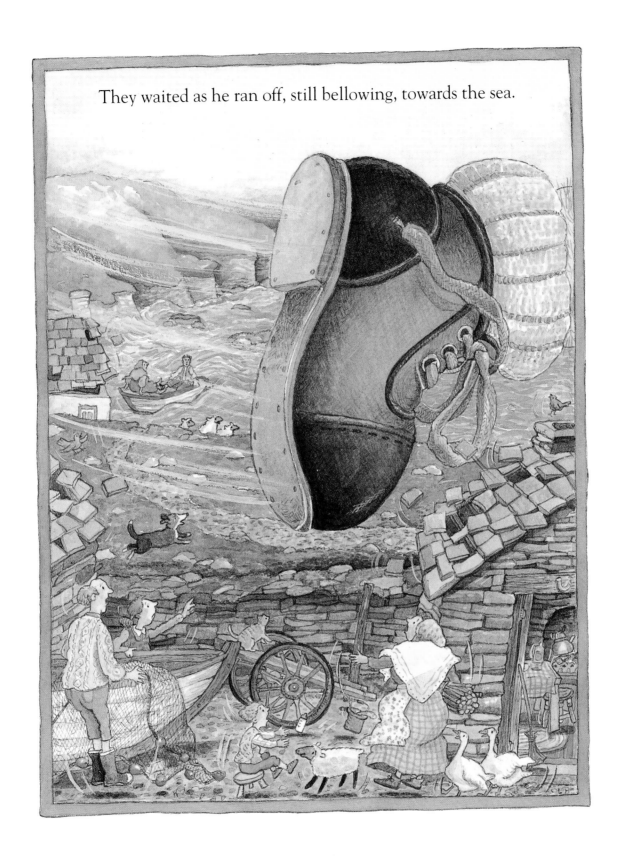

25

Then Finn began to giggle. He couldn't stop it once he started, and soon he was shaking so much that the cradle broke and he ended up on the floor.

But Finn didn't care a pin. He got up, took his wife in his arms and danced her all around the nursery until they hardly had any breath left.

"You're the finest woman in all Ireland," he gasped as he finally let her go. Sara had saved his life, his castle and the kingdom. The King and everybody else would still think he was the bravest giant of all. What's more, Sara had given Fergus such a scare, Finn knew he would never bother them again. And, to be sure, Fergus never did.

Finn MacCoul and Sara went on to live to a ripe old age in great happiness together. The only sign of Fergus's historic visit is part of the stone bridge he built, which stands by the edge of the sea to this very day.

If you ever go to Ireland or to Scotland, you can see the remains of
The Giant's Causeway for yourself. And if you listen carefully, you
may still hear the giants' echoes rumbling in the sounds of the
ever-rolling sea.

THE END

Oxford University Press, 70 Wynford Drive, Don Mills, Ontario, M3C 1J9

Toronto Oxford New York Delhi Bombay Calcutta Madras Karachi
Petaling Jaya Singapore Hong Kong Tokyo Nairobi Dar es Salaam
Cape Town Melbourne Auckland

and associated companies in

Berlin Ibadan

Canadian Cataloguing in Publication Data

Harpur, Tom
The terrible Finn MacCoul

ISBN 0-19-540716-4

1. Finn MacCumhaill, 3rd cent. - Legends.
2. Legends - Ireland. I. Hendry, Linda.
II. Title.

PS8565.A77T47 1990   j398.2'2'09415   C89-094822-4
PZ8.1.H376Te 1990

Text © Tom Harpur 1990
Illustrations © Linda Hendry 1990

Oxford is a trademark of Oxford University Press

1 2 3 4 - 3 2 1 0

Printed in Singapore